ELEMENTS OF POETRY

Elements of Poetry

ROBERT SCHOLES

New York
OXFORD UNIVERSITY PRESS
London   Toronto   1969

For Birdo, who knows how poetry feels

CONTENTS

ELEMENTS OF POETRY

PART ONE

INTRODUCTION

THE POETRY GAME

If you ask a poet, "What good is it? I mean, what earthly good is it?" you may get an answer like Marianne Moore's:

> I, too, dislike it

or W. H. Auden's:

> poetry makes nothing happen.

The modern poet is not likely to make grandiose claims for his craft. And I will try not to betray that honest and tough-minded attitude. When T. S. Eliot called poetry "a superior amusement" he said it all, so far as I am concerned. Poetry is essentially a game, with artificial rules, and it takes two—a writer and a reader— to play it. If the reader is reluctant, the game will not work.

Physical games have their practical aspects. They help make sound bodies to go with the sound minds so admired by philosophers of education. A language game like poetry also has uses which are by-products of it rather than its proper ends. Poetry exercises a valuable though perhaps "unsound" side of the mind: imagination. (It takes an exercise of the imagination, for example, to get at what Bob Dylan means by a "hard rain.") Poetry can also be used to develop the student's ability to control and respond to language. But it is a game first of all, where—as Robert Frost said—"the work is play for mortal stakes." A game can require great exertion, but it must reward that exertion with pleasure or there is no playing it. Anyone who has ever responded to a nursery rhyme, or to a Beatles record, or to Pete Seeger singing a ballad has experienced the fundamental pleasure of poetry. More complicated and sophisticated poems offer essentially the same kind of pleasure. We labor to understand the rules of the game so that we need not think about them when we are playing. We master technique to make our execution easier. When we are really proficient the work becomes play.

THE QUALITIES OF POETRY

Part of the pleasure of poetry lies in its relationship to music. It awakens in us a fundamental response to rhythmic repetitions of various kinds. Learning to read poetry is partly a matter of learning to respond to subtle and delicate rhythmic patterns as well as the most obvious and persistant ones. But poetry is not just a kind of music. It is a special combination of musical and linguistic qualities—of sounds regarded both as pure sound and as meaningful speech. In particular, poetry is expressive language. It does for us what Samuel Beckett's character Watt wanted done for him:

> Not that Watt desired information, for he did not. But he desired words to be applied to his situation, to Mr Knott, to the house, to the grounds, to his duties, to the stairs, to his bedroom, to the kitchen, and in a general way to the conditions of being in which he found himself.

Poetry applies words to our situations, to the conditions of being in which we find ourselves. By doing so, it gives us pleasure because it helps us articulate our states of mind. The poets we value are important because they speak for us and help us learn to speak for ourselves. A revealing instance of a poet learning to apply words to his own situation, and finding in their order and symmetry a soothing pleasure, has been recorded by James Joyce. Here we can see a child of nine years making an important discovery about the nature and uses of poetry:*

* Quoted in *The Workshop of Daedalus*, by Robert Scholes and Richard Kain, Evanston, 1965. Reprinted by permission of The Society of Authors.

[Bray: in the parlour of the house
in Martello Terrace]

Mr Vance—(*comes in with a stick*). . . O, you know,
    he'll have to apologise, Mrs Joyce.

Mrs Joyce—O yes . . . Do you hear that, Jim?

Mr Vance—Or else—if he doesn't—the eagles'll
    come and pull out his eyes

Mrs Joyce—O, but I'm sure he will apologise.

Joyce—(*under the table, to himself*)

    —Pull out his eyes,
    Apologise,
    Apologise,
    Pull out his eyes.

    Apologise,
    Pull out his eyes,
    Pull out his eyes,
    Apologise.

The coincidence of sound which links the four-word
phrase "pull-out-his-eyes" with the four-syllable word
"apologise" offers the child a refuge from Mr Vance
far more secure than the table under which he is hiding.
Joyce used this moment from his own life in his novel
A Portrait of the Artist as a Young Man to illustrate
Stephen's vocation for verbal art.

As a poem the child's effort is of course a simple one,
but it makes a real effect because of the contrast between the meanings of its two basic lines which sound
so much alike. Gentle "apologise" and fierce "pull out

his eyes" ought not to fit together so neatly, the poem implies, and in doing so it makes an ethical criticism of Mr Vance, who, after all, coupled them in the first place. Young Joyce's deliberate wit has made a poem from the old man's witless tirade.

Marianne Moore qualifies her dislike of poetry this way:*

I, too, dislike it: there are things that are important beyond
    all this fiddle.
  Reading it, however, with a perfect contempt for it, one
    discovers in
it after all, a place for the genuine.
    Hands that can grasp, eyes
    that can dilate, hair that can rise
      if it must, these things are important not because a

high-sounding interpretation can be put upon them but
    because they are
  useful. . . .

* From *The Collected Poems of* Marianne Moore. Copyright 1935 by Marianne Moore. Renewed 1963 by Marianne Moore and T. S. Eliot. Reprinted by permission of The Macmillan Company and Faber and Faber, Ltd. In the latest version of this poem (1967), Miss Moore has eliminated all but a few lines of the earlier text, so that the complete poem reads:

  I, too, dislike it.
    Reading it, however, with a perfect contempt for it,
                    one discovers in
    it after all, a place for the genuine.

And Auden adds,*

> . . . poetry makes nothing happen: it survives
> In the valley of its saying where executives
> Would never want to tamper; it flows south
> From ranches of isolation and the busy griefs,
> Raw towns that we believe and die in; it survives,
> A way of happening, a mouth.

He concludes the poem from which these lines are taken with some advice to poets that suggests the kinds of thing poetry can do:

> Follow, poet, follow right
> To the bottom of the night,
> With your unconstraining voice
> Still persuade us to rejoice;
>
> With the farming of a verse
> Make a vineyard of the curse,
> Sing of human unsuccess
> In a rapture of distress;
>
> In the deserts of the heart
> Let the healing fountain start,
> In the prison of his days
> Teach the free man how to praise.

* From "In Memory of W. B. Yeats," by W. H. Auden. Copyright 1940 by W. H. Auden. Reprinted from *Collected Shorter Poems 1927–1957* by W. H. Auden, by permission of Random House, Inc. and Faber and Faber, Ltd.

Poetry, then, is a kind of musical word game which we value because of its expressive qualities. Not all poems are equally musical, or equally playful, or equally expressive. Nor are they necessarily musical, playful, or expressive in the same way. But we can consider these three qualities as the basic constituents of poetry so that we may examine some of the various ways in which poets combine and modify them in making different kinds of poems. Recognizing various poetic possibilities is important to the student of poetry because the greatest single problem for the reader of a poem is the problem of tact.

TACT

Tact acknowledges the diversity of poetry. A tactful approach to a poem must be appropriate to the special nature of the poem under consideration. Reading a poem for the first time ought to be a little like meeting a person for the first time. An initial exploratory conversation may lead to friendship, dislike, indifference, or any of dozens of other shades of attitude from love to hate. If the relationship progresses, it will gain in intimacy as surface politeness is replaced by exchange of ideas and feelings at a deeper level.

We need, of course, to speak the same language if we are to communicate in any serious way. For most of us, this means we make friends with people who speak English and we read poems written in English. But

speaking the same language means more than just in-
heriting or acquiring the same linguistic patterns. Some
poems, like some people, seem to talk to us not merely
in our native language but in our own idiom as well.
We understand them easily and naturally. Others speak
in ways that seem strange and puzzling. With poems,
as with people, our first response to the puzzling should
be a polite effort to eliminate misunderstanding. We
need not adopt any false reverence before the poems of
earlier ages. An old poem may be as much of a bore as
an old person. But we should treat the aged with genuine politeness, paying attention to their words, trying
to adjust to their idiom. This may turn out to be very
rewarding, or it may not. But only after we have understood are we entitled to reject—or accept—any utterance.

Since the English language itself has changed con-
siderably over the centuries and continues to change,
we must often make a greater effort to understand an
older poem than a modern one. Also, notions of what
poetry is and should be have changed in the past and
continue to change. The poetry game has not always
been played with the same linguistic equipment or
under the same rules. The difference between a love
lyric by an Elizabethan sonneteer and a contemporary
poem of love may be as great as the difference between
Elizabethan tennis and modern tennis. The Elizabethans
played tennis indoors, in an intricately walled court
which required great finesse to master all its angles.

The modern game is flat and open, all power serves and rushes to the net. Which ought to remind us that Robert Frost likened free verse to playing tennis with the net down. Such a game would make points easy to score but would not be much fun to play. Poetry, like tennis, depends on artificial rules and hindrances. These arbitrary restrictions are what give it its game-like quality.

Unlike the rules of tennis, however, the rules of poetry have never really been written down. Although critics have frequently tried to produce a "poetics" which would operate like a code of rules, they have always failed because poetry is always changing. In fact poetic "rules" are not really rules but conventions which change perpetually and must change perpetually to prevent poems from being turned out on a mass scale according to formulas. Every poet learns from his predecessors, but any poet who merely imitates them produces flat, stale poems. A poet is above all a man who finds a unique idiom, a special voice for his own poetry. The tactful reader quickly picks up the conventions operating in any particular poem and pays careful attention to the idiom of every poet, so that he can understand and appreciate or criticize each separate poetic performance.

The following sections of this book are designed to help the student of poetry to acquire tact. They are arranged to present certain basic elements drawn from the whole system of poetic conventions. Tact itself cannot be taught because it is of the spirit. But if the instinct for it is there, tact can be developed and refined through conscious effort. In the pages that follow, the student may consider consciously and deliberately the kinds of intellectual and emotional adjustments that the expert reader of poetry makes effortlessly and instantaneously.

PART TWO

EXPRESSION

DRAMA AND NARRATION

Drama usually implies actors on a stage impersonating characters who speak to one another in a sequence of situations or scenes. A short poem with a single speaker, thus, is dramatic only in a limited sense. Nevertheless, *some* poems are very dramatic; the element of drama in them must be grasped if we are to understand them at all. And *all* poems are dramatic to some extent, however slight.

We approach the dramatic element in poetry by assuming that every poem shares some qualities with a speech in a play: that it is spoken aloud by a "speaker" who is a character in a situation which implies a certain relationship with other characters; and we assume that this speech is "overheard" by an audience. We may have to modify these assumptions. The poem may finally be more like a soliloquy or unspoken thought than like a part of a dialogue. Or it may seem more like a letter or a song than a speech. Still, in beginning our approach to a poem we must make some sort of tentative decision about who the speaker is, what his situation is, and who he seems to be addressing. In poems which are especially dramatic, the interest of the poem will depend on the interest of the character and situation presented. But because dramatic poems are very short and compressed in comparison with plays, the reader must usually do a good deal of guessing or inferring in order to grasp the elements of character and situation. The good reader will make plausible inferences; the inadequate reader will guess wildly, breaking the rules of plausibility and spoiling the inferential game. Consider the following lines from the beginning of a dramatic poem. This imaginary speech is assigned by the title of the poem to a painter who lived in Renaissance Italy. Brother Filippo Lippi was a Carmelite friar and an important painter, whose work was sponsored by the rich and powerful Florentine banker Cosimo di Medici.

FRA LIPPO LIPPI

I AM poor brother Lippo, by your leave!
You need not clap your torches to my face.
Zooks, what 's to blame? you think you see a monk!
What, 't is past midnight, and you go the rounds,
And here you catch me at an alley's end   5
Where sportive ladies leave their doors ajar?
The Carmine 's my cloister: hunt it up,
Do,—harry out, if you must show your zeal,

Whatever rat, there, haps on his wrong hole,
And nip each softling of a wee white mouse,   10
Weke, weke, that 's crept to keep him company!
Aha, you know your betters! Then, you 'll take
Your hand away that 's fiddling on my throat,
And please to know me likewise. Who am I?
Why, one, sir, who is lodging with a friend   15
Three streets off—he 's a certain . . . how d' ye call?
Master—a . . . Cosimo of the Medici,
I' the house that caps the corner. Boh! you were best!
Remember and tell me, the day you 're hanged,
How you affected such a gullet's-gripe!   20
But you, sir, it concerns you that your knaves
Pick up a manner nor discredit you:
Zooks, are we pilchards, that they sweep the streets
And count fair prize what comes into their net?
He 's Judas to a tittle, that man is!   25
Just such a face! Why, sir, you make amends.
Lord, I 'm not angry! Bid your hangdogs go
Drink out this quarter-florin to the health
Of the munificent House that harbours me
(And many more beside, lads! more beside!)   30
And all 's come square again. I 'd like his face—
His, elbowing on his comrade in the door
With the pike and lantern,—for the slave that holds
John Baptist's head a-dangle by the hair
With one hand ("Look, you, now," as who should say)   35
And his weapon in the other, yet unwiped!
It 's not your chance to have a bit of chalk,

A wood-coal or the like? or you should see!
Yes, I 'm the painter, since you style me so.

Now consider, in order, each of these questions:

1. From these lines, what can we infer about the situation and its development?
2. Who is Lippo speaking to in the opening lines?
3. At what time of day and in what sort of neighborhood does this scene take place?
4. Would we be justified in making an inference about what Lippo has been up to? What inference might we make?
5. What is Lippo talking about when he says in line 18, "Boh! you were best!"? And who does he say it to? What produced the action which Lippo refers to here?
6. In line 21 he addresses a different person in "you, sir." Who is he addressing?
7. What kind of man do the details in these lines suggest is speaking in this poem?
8. How would you describe the whole progress of the situation? How might the events presented in these 39 lines be re-told in the form of a story narrated by an observer of the action?

This series of questions—and their answers—should suggest the kind of inferential activity that many dramatic poems require of their readers. The words of such a poem are points of departure, and the actual poem is the one we create with our imaginative but logical response to the poet's words. The poet—Robert Browning—offers us the pleasure of helping to create his poem, and also the pleasure of entering a world remote from our own in time and space. Dramatic poems like Browning's do not so much apply words to our situations as take us out of ourselves into situations beyond our experience. When we speak Lippo's words aloud, or read them imaginatively, we are refreshed by this assumption of a strange role and this expression of a personality other than our own. In a sense, our minds are expanded, and we return to ourselves enriched by the experience. Yet even the strangest characters will often express ideas and attitudes which we recognize as related to our own, related to certain moods or conditions of being in which we have found ourselves. Every citizen who has had to explain an awkward situation to a policeman has something in common with Lippo Lippi as he begins to speak.

The line between the dramatic and narrative elements in a poem is not always clear. But a narrative poem gives us a story as told by a narrator from a perspective outside the action, while a dramatic poem presents a fragment of an action (or story) through the voice (or point of view) of a character involved in that action. The principal speaker in a narrative poem addresses us —the audience—directly, telling us about the situation and perhaps offering us introductions to characters who function as dramatic elements in the poem. In the days when long stories were recited aloud by bardic poets, verse was the natural form for narration, because it provided easily memorizable units of composition and a regular, flowing rhythm into which these units might be fitted. But now that printing has converted most of the audience for fiction from listeners to readers, most stories are told in prose. The only narrative verse form that is really alive today is the ballad, which justifies its use of rhyme and rhythm by being set to music and sung. Verse meant to be sung has its own rules or conventions, which will be discussed later on. But here we can talk about the narrative element in ballads and other forms of fiction in verse, and how versified fiction differs from the kind of story we expect to find in prose.

If we think of a dramatic poem as something like a self-sufficient fragment torn from a play, which through its compression encourages us to fill out its dramatic frame by acts of inference and imagination—then we may think of a narrative poem as related to prose fiction in a similar way. In comparison to stories, narrative poems are compressed and eliptical, shifting their focus, concentrating on striking details, and leaving us to make appropriate connections and draw appropriate conclusions. In fact, there is a strong tendency toward the dramatic in short verse narratives—a tendency to present more dialogue or action in relation to description than we would expect to find in prose fiction dealing with the same subject matter.

Actually, we find poetic elements in much prose fiction and fictional elements in many poems. (The elements of fiction have been treated in another book in this series.) Here we are concerned mainly with the special problems posed by the compressed and eliptical form taken by fiction in short poems such as this one:*

REUBEN BRIGHT

Because he was a butcher and thereby
Did earn an honest living (and did right)
I would not have you think that Reuben Bright
Was any more a brute than you or I;
For when they told him that his wife must die,
He stared at them, and shook with grief and fright,
And cried like a great baby half that night,
And made the women cry to see him cry.

And after she was dead, and he had paid
The singers and the sexton and the rest,
He packed a lot of things that she had made
Most mournfully away in an old chest
Of hers, and put some chopped-up cedar boughs
In with them, and tore down the slaughter-house.

The poem is narrative because the speaker addresses us from a perspective outside the action and undertakes to comment for our benefit on the character and situa-

* From *The Children of the Night*, 1897, by Edward Arlington Robinson, reprinted by permission of Macmillan & Co., Ltd.

tion presented: Reuben earns an "honest" living; he
did "right." Yet the narrator presents just two incidents
from the whole of Bright's life, and he makes no final
interpretation or commentary on Bright's climactic act.
It is left for us to conclude that only by destroying the
place of butchery could this butcher express his an-
guish at the death of his beloved wife. And it is left for
us to note the irony involved in this presentation of an
act of destructive violence as evidence that the butcher
is not "any more a brute than you or I." It is also left
for us to note the pathos of this gesture by which the
butcher tries to dissociate himself from that death
which has claimed his wife. The compactness and brevity characteristic of poetry often move narration in the
direction of drama.

Consider the combination of drama and narration in
the following poem:*

PIANO

Softly, in the dusk, a woman is singing to me;
Taking me back down the vista of years, till I see
A child sitting under the piano, in the boom of the tingling
      strings

* From *The Complete Poems of D. H. Lawrence*, edited by
Vivian de Sola Pinto and F. Warren Roberts. Copyright 1920
by B. W. Huebsch, Inc., renewed 1948 by Frieda Lawrence. Reprinted by permission of The Viking Press, Inc. and Lawrence
Pollinger, Ltd.

And pressing the small, poised feet of a mother who smiles
   as she sings.

In spite of myself, the insidious mastery of song
Betrays me back, till the heart of me weeps to belong
To the old Sunday evenings at home, with winter outside
And hymns in the cosy parlour, the tinkling piano our
   guide.

So now it is vain for the singer to burst into clamour
With the great black piano appassionato. The glamour
Of childish days is upon me, my manhood is cast
Down in the flood of remembrance, I weep like a child for
   the past.

Here the speaker seems to be addressing us directly
as a narrator. But he is describing a scene in which he
is the central character, and describing it in the present
tense as something in progress. Drama is always *now*.
Narrative is always *then*. But this scene mingles now
and then, bringing together two pianos, and two pian-
ists; linking the speaker's childish self with his present
manhood. In a sense, the poem depends on its combination of now and then, drama and narration, for its
effect—uniting now and then, man and child, in its
last clause: "I weep like a child for the past." Because
this is a poem, tightly compressed, it is possible for us
to miss an essential aspect of the dramatic situation it
presents. Why is it "vain" for the singer to play the

piano "appassionato"? Why does he say that his "man-hood" is cast down? What does this phrase mean? These eliptical references seem intended to suggest that the woman at the piano is in some sense wooing the man who listens, attempting to arouse his passion through her performance. But ironically, she only reminds him of his mother, casting down his manhood, reducing him from a lover to a son, from a man to a child.

I find it interesting to compare this poem by D. H. Lawrence to an early version of it. Looking at the early draft, we might consider Lawrence's revisions as an attempt to achieve a more satisfactory combination of narrative and drama, and a more intense poem. The early version tells quite a different story from the later one—almost the opposite story. And it contains much that Lawrence eliminated. Examine the revisions in detail. What does each change accomplish? Which changes are most important, most effective?*

THE PIANO [Early Version]

Somewhere beneath that piano's superb sleek black
Must hide my mother's piano, little and brown, with the
     back

That stood close to the wall, and the front's faded silk both
    torn,
And the keys with little hollows, that my mother's fingers
    had worn.

Softly, in the shadows, a woman is singing to me
Quietly, through the years I have crept back to see
A child sitting under the piano, in the boom of the shaking
    strings
Pressing the little poised feet of the mother who smiles as
    she sings.

The full throated woman has chosen a winning, living song
And surely the heart that is in me must belong
To the old Sunday evenings, when darkness wandered
    outside
And hymns gleamed on our warm lips, as we watched
    mother's fingers glide.

Or this is my sister at home in the old front room
Singing love's first surprised gladness, alone in the gloom.
She will start when she sees me, and blushing, spread out
    her hands
To cover my mouth's raillery, till I'm bound in her shame's
    heartspun bands.

A woman is singing me a wild Hungarian air
And her arms, and her bosom, and the whole of her soul is
    bare,

And the great black piano is clamouring as my mother's
    never could clamour
And my mother's tunes are devoured of this music's ravag-
    ing glamour.

DESCRIPTION AND MEDITATION

Description is the element in poetry closest to painting
and sculpture. Poets like Edmund Spenser, Keats, and
Tennyson have been very sensitive to this relationship:
Spenser maintained that the Poet's wit "passeth Painter
farre," while Keats admitted that a painted piece of
Greek pottery could "express a flowery tale more sweetly
than our rhyme." In fact, describing with words has
both advantages and disadvantages in comparison to
plastic representation. Words are rich in meaning and
suggestion but weak for rendering precise spatial relationships and shades of color. Therefore, what descriptive words do best is convey an attitude or feeling
through the objects which they describe. Take a very
simple description from a short poem by William
Carlos Williams:*

                    a red wheel
                    barrow

* From "So much Depends" by William Carlos Williams. From
Collected Earlier Poems by William Carlos Williams. Copyright
1938 by William Carlos Williams. Reprinted by permission of
New Directions Publishing Corporation and MacGibbon and
Kee.

> glazed with rain
> water
>
> beside the white
> chickens.

We sense a word game here in the arbitrary arrangement of the words in lines, as they lead us to consider
a visual image dominated by contrasting colors and
textures—feathery white and glazed red, animate and
inaminate things. But it is hard to sense clearly any
attitude conveyed by the description, which seems like
a poor substitute for a painting. Here is the entire
poem:

> so much depends
> upon
>
> a red wheel
> barrow
>
> glazed with rain
> water
>
> beside the white
> chickens.

Now we can see how the description itself depends
upon the assertion "so much depends" for its animation. The assertion directs our search for meaning, and
conveys the speaker's attitude toward the objects described. We may wonder how anything at all can

"depend" on such insignificant objects, but this very response is a response not just to a description but to a poem. The poem is created by the distance between this sweeping statement and the apparent insignificance of the objects it refers to. We understand, finally, that the poet is using this distance to make us feel his concern for trivial things, his sense that there is beauty in humble objects; and beyond that he is encouraging us to share his alertness to the beautful in things that are neither artful nor conventionally pretty. He is advising us to keep our eyes open, and he does it not with a direct admonition but with a description charged with the vigor of his own response to the visible world.

It is of the essence of poetic description that it come to us charged with the poet's feelings and attitudes. Sometimes these will be made explicit by statement or commentary in the poem. Sometimes they will remain implicit, matters of tone, rhythm, and metaphor. Consider these four opening lines from a poem by Tennyson. What attitudes or emotions are conveyed by them, and how are they conveyed?

> The woods decay, the woods decay and fall,
> The vapours weep their burthen to the ground,
> Man comes and tills the field and lies beneath,
> And after many a summer dies the swan.

The topic is decay and death, presented in terms of generalized natural description. In line 1 the continuing process of decay is emphasized by the exact repetition of a whole clause. In line 2 the vapours are presented as sentient creatures who weep. In line 3 the whole adult life of man is compressed into just nine words, few seconds, a patch of earth. In the climactic position, reserved by an inversion of normal syntax for the very last place in the sentence, comes the death of the swan. The life and death of man is thus surrounded by decay and death in other natural things, and in this way is reduced, distanced. It is not horrible but natural, and characterized by a melancholy beauty.

These lines of description serve in the poem as the beginning of a dramatic monologue. The nature of the speaker and his situation (as we come to understand them) help us to refine our grasp of the tone and the attitude these lines convey toward the objects they describe. Here is the opening verse-paragraph of the poem:

TITHONUS

The woods decay, the woods decay and fall,
The vapours weep their burthen to the ground,
Man comes and tills the field and lies beneath,
And after many a summer dies the swan.
Me only cruel immortality   5
Consumes: I wither slowly in thine arms,
Here at the quiet limit of the world,
A white-haired shadow roaming like a dream
The ever-silent spaces of the East,
Far-folded mists, and gleaming halls of morn.   10

The speaker is Tithonus, a mythological prince who became the lover of the dawn goddess; she made him immortal but could not prevent him from growing older throughout eternity. In the light of lines 5 and 6, the first four lines are enriched with the wistful envy of one who is unable to die. At the close of the poem (some seventy lines later) the speaker returns to the images of line 3 in speaking of "happy men that have the power to die" and of "the grassy barrows of the happier dead." He asks for release so that he can become "earth in earth" and forget his unhappy existence. The melancholy beauty of the opening lines becomes more lovely and less sad as we move toward the conclusion of the poem with its powerful projection of man's return to earth as the most desirable of consummations. Behind the dramatic speaker in the poem— the mythological Tithonus—stands the poet, reminding us that death is natural and the appropriate end of life. In this poem, description and drama collaborate to suggest rather than state a meaning.

Serious English poetry has often embodied in particular poems a movement from description to overt meditation. This movement is frequently found in religious poetry, as poets move from contemplation of created things to an awareness of the Creator. William Wordsworth was a master—perhaps *the* master—of this kind of poetic movement in English. Thus, a substantial selection from Wordsworth makes a fitting

culmination to this discussion of description and meditation. These lines from Wordsworth are presented
with a minimum of commentary, so that the student
may make his own analysis of them. But to facilitate
that analysis, some directions for inquiry have been
appended at the end of the passage. The lines that follow are not really a complete poem but can be read as
one. They are the opening 129 lines of Book XIV of
The Prelude, Wordsworth's poetic autobiography.

In one of those excursions (may they ne'er
Fade from remembrance!) through the Northern tracts
Of Cambria ranging with a youthful friend,
I left Bethgelert's huts at couching-time,
And westward took my way, to see the sun   5
Rise, from the top of Snowdon. To the door
Of a rude cottage at the mountain's base
We came, and roused the shepherd who attends
The adventurous stranger's steps, a trusty guide;
Then, cheered by short refreshment, sallied forth.   10

   It was a close, warm, breezeless summer night,
Wan, dull, and glaring, with a dripping fog
Low-hung and thick that covered all the sky;
But, undiscouraged, we began to climb
The mountain-side. The mist soon girt us round,   15
And, after ordinary travellers' talk
With our conductor, pensively we sank
Each into commerce with his private thoughts:

Thus did we breast the ascent, and by myself
Was nothing either seen or heard that checked   20
Those musings or diverted, save that once
The shepherd's lurcher, who, among the crags,
Had to his joy unearthed a hedgehog, teased
His coiled-up prey with barkings turbulent.
This small adventure, for even such it seemed   25
In that wild place and at the dead of night,
Being over and forgotten, on we wound
In silence as before. With forehead bent
Earthward, as if in opposition set
Against an enemy, I panted up   30
With eager pace, and no less eager thoughts.
Thus might we wear a midnight hour away,
Ascending at loose distance each from each,
And I, as chanced, the foremost of the band;
When at my feet the ground appeared to brighten,   35
And with a step or two seemed brighter still;
Nor was time given to ask or learn the cause,
For instantly a light upon the turf
Fell like a flash, and lo! as I looked up,
The Moon hung naked in a firmament   40
Of azure without cloud, and at my feet
Rested a silent sea of hoary mist.
A hundred hills their dusky backs upheaved
All over this still ocean; and beyond,
Far, far beyond, the solid vapours stretched,   45
In headlands, tongues, and promontory shapes,
Into the main Atlantic, that appeared

To dwindle, and give up his majesty,
Usurped upon far as the sight could reach.
Not so the ethereal vault; encroachment none   50
Was there, nor loss; only the inferior stars
Had disappeared, or shed a fainter light
In the clear presence of the full-orbed Moon,
Who, from her sovereign elevation, gazed
Upon the billowy ocean, as it lay   55
All meek and silent, save that through a rift—
Not distant from the shore whereon we stood,
A fixed, abysmal, gloomy, breathing-place—
Mounted the roar of water, torrents, streams
Innumerable, roaring with one voice!   60
Heard over earth and sea, and, in that hour,
For so it seemed, felt by the starry heavens.

    When into air had partially dissolved
That vision, given to spirits of the night
And three chance human wanderers, in calm thought   65
Reflected, it appeared to me the type
Of a majestic intellect, its acts
And its possessions, what it has and craves,
What in itself it is, and would become.
There I beheld the emblem of a mind   70
That feeds upon infinity, that broods
Over the dark abyss, intent to hear
Its voices issuing forth to silent light
In one continuous stream; a mind sustained
By recognitions of transcendent power,   75

In sense conducting to ideal form,
In soul of more than mortal privilege.
One function, above all, of such a mind
Had Nature shadowed there, by putting forth,
'Mid circumstances awful and sublime,   80
That mutual domination which she loves
To exert upon the face of outward things,
So moulded, joined, abstracted, so endowed
With interchangeable supremacy,
That men, least sensitive, see, hear, perceive,   85
And cannot choose but feel. The power, which all
Acknowledge when thus moved, which Nature thus
To bodily sense exhibits, is the express
Resemblance of that glorious faculty
That higher minds bear with them as their own.   90
This is the very spirit in which they deal
With the whole compass of the universe:
They from their native selves can send abroad
Kindred mutations; for themselves create
A like existence; and, whene'er it dawns   95
Created for them, catch it, or are caught
By its inevitable mastery,
Like angels stopped upon the wing by sound
Of harmony from Heaven's remotest spheres.
Them the enduring and the transient both   100
Serve to exalt; they build up greatest things
From least suggestions; ever on the watch,
Willing to work and to be wrought upon,
They need not extraordinary calls

To rouse them; in a world of life they live,   105
By sensible impressions not enthralled,
But by their quickening impulse made more prompt
To hold fit converse with the spiritual world,
And with the generations of mankind
Spread over time, past, present, and to come,   110
Age after age, till Time shall be no more.
Such minds are truly from the Deity,
For they are Powers; and hence the highest bliss
That flesh can know is theirs—the consciousness
Of Whom they are, habitually infused   115
Through every image and through every thought,
And all affections by communion raised
From earth to heaven, from human to divine;
Hence endless occupation for the Soul,
Whether discursive or intuitive;   120
Hence cheerfulness for acts of daily life,
Emotions which best foresight need not fear,
Most worthy then of trust when most intense.
Hence, amid ills that vex and wrongs that crush
Our hearts—if here the words of Holy Writ   125
May with fit reverence be applied—that peace
Which passeth understanding, that repose
In moral judgments which from this pure source
Must come, or will by man be sought in vain.

After line 10 the passage is divided into two sections.
The first is essentially descriptive and the second meditative. Questions:

1. In what ways are the two sections related?

2. How is the description section organized? Does it have a necessary order or "plot"?

3. In lines 40 to 62, how does Wordsworth convey his feeling that natural objects have a kind of sentient existence?

4. In the meditative section Wordsworth first suggests that this natural secene is the "type" (line 66) or "emblem" (line 70) of a divine mind. Then he suggests that Nature has in particular presented in this scene ("shadowed there") "one function" of such a mind. What is the function?

5. Consider the sentence in lines 86–90. How is the "power" in line 86 related to the "function" of line 78?

6. How is the "glorious faculty" of line 89 related to the "power" of line 86?

7. Who are the "higher minds" of line 90?

8. Lines 91–129 elaborate on the qualities of that "glorious faculty." What are these qualities?

9. Can you find an appropriate name or names for the glorious faculty?

10. Return to question 1 and answer it more fully.

PART THREE

WORD GAMES

Language can be used to help us perceive relationships which connect disparate things, or to help us make discriminations which separate similar things. In poetry these two aspects of language take the form of metaphorical comparison and ironic contrast. Metaphor and irony are the twin bases of poetical language. This means that a good reader of poetry must be especially alert and tactful in his responses to metaphorical and ironic language.

It is because poetry places such stress on these crucial dimensions of language that it is of such great use in developing linguistic skills in its readers. It makes unusual demands and offers unusual rewards. The kind of skill it takes to be a first rate reader of poetry cannot be acquired by reading a handbook like this one, any more than the ability to play the piano can be acquired in a few lessons. Continuing practice is the most important factor in a performing art like piano-playing, and reading poetry (even silently, to oneself) has many of the qualities and satisfactions of a performing art.

In the sections that follow on metaphoric and ironic language, I have not tried to present an exhaustive list of poetical devices to be carefully noted and memorized. I have tried to examine some of the main varieties of metaphoric and ironic language, with a view toward establishing an awareness of these two crucial varieties of poetical word-play. To move from awareness to expertise, the student must read many poems and talk about them with an understanding instructor. In time, he may become impatient with the simple distinctions and terminology employed here. Until then, they may be of use.

SOME VARIETIES OF METAPHORICAL LANGUAGE

Simile. This is the easiest form of metaphor to perceive because in it both of the images or ideas being joined are stated and explicity linked by the word *as* or *like* or a similar linking-word. Similes are often quite simple:

> O my Love's like a red, red rose

But even a statement of resemblance as simple and direct as this one of Robert Burns' asks us to consider the ways in which his beloved is like a rose—and not a white or yellow rose, but a red rose. And not just a red rose but a "red, red" rose. What the redness of the rose has to do with the qualities of the speaker's beloved is the first question this simile poses for us. In the poem, the simile is further complicated by a second line:

> O my Love's like a red, red rose,
> That's newly sprung in June;

Here we are asked to associate the freshness of the flower and its early blooming with the qualities of the speaker's beloved. In the poem, the next two lines add a second image, compounding the simile:

> O my Love's like the melodie
> That's sweetly played in tune.

The first image emphasizes the spontaneous naturalness of the beloved, the second her harmonious composure. Both roses and sweet melodies are pleasing; so that, in a sense, the poet is using his similies to make the simple statement that his beloved is pleasing to behold. But the simile is also saying that she has a complicated kind of appeal: like the rose, to sight and smell; like the melody, to the sense of sound; like the rose, a natural fresh quality; like the melody, a deliberate artfulness which intends to please. The simile also conveys to us the strength of the poet's feeling; his choice of images tells us something about the qualities of his feeling for her, because it is *he* who has found these words—which themselves have some of qualities of spontaneous freshness and tuneful order.

A single simile can also be elaborated: as in the traditional epic simile, in which the illustrative image is often extensive enough to require the construction *as . . . so*, or *like . . . thus*. An extended simile, by multiplying possible points of contact between the thing presented and the illustrative image, can often become very complicated indeed, with the illustrative image itself becoming a thing to be illustrated or developed with other images still. Consider, for example, this epic simile from Book IV of Spenser's *Faerie Queene:*

27

Like as the tide that comes from th' Ocean main,
Flows up the Shanon with contrary force,
And overruling him in his own reign,
Drives back the current of his kindly course,
And makes it seem to have some other source:
But when the flood is spent, then back again
His borrowed waters forced to redisbourse
He sends the sea his own with double gain
And tribute eke withall, as to his Soveraine.

28

Thus did the battle vary to and fro . . .

Metaphor. The word metaphor is used both as a general term for all kinds of poetic linking of images and ideas, and as a specific term for such linking when the thing and image are not presented as a direct analogy (A is *like* B) but by discussing one in terms of the other (A *is* B-ish, or A B's; Albert *is* a dog or Albert *barked* at me). For example, within the epic simile from Spenser, we can find metaphor at work. The simile involves describing a hand-to-hand combat in terms of the ebb and flow of tides where the River Shanon meets the Atlantic Ocean. The ebb and flow of the waters illustrates the shifting tide of battle (as this metaphor become a cliché usually puts it). But this basic simile in Spenser is enriched by the idea of Shanon and Ocean as hostile potentates engaged in a struggle, with the Ocean tide invading the river and "overruling him in his own reign." The struggle of potentates is itself further complicated by a financial metaphor. The phrase "when the flood is spent" means literally when the incoming tide has expended its force and lost its momentum. But Spenser chooses to use the financial overtones in the word "spent" to further adorn his metaphor. From "spent" he moves to "borrowed" and "redisburse," and the concept of repayment with 100 per cent interest in the expression "double gain." This transaction between Ocean and Shanon can be seen as a combat or a loan. Finally, Spenser merges these two metaphors in the last line of the stanza, by calling this double payment the "tribute" of a lesser feudal power to a higher. And here Spenser actually turns his metaphor into a simile within the basic simile, with the expression "*as* to his Soveraine."

This kind of interweaving of similes and metaphors

is playful and decorative in its intent. The metaphors
seem to emerge naturally and blend easily with one
another. But these graceful arabesques tell us nothing
much about the course of the combat of the two war-
riors, beyond the suggestion that the fight ebbs and
flows. Their struggle is not so much described as dig-
nified by this heroic comparison to two sovereign forces
of nature.

In poems which depend heavily on metaphoric proc-
esses for their interest, the subtle interaction of images
and ideas almost defies analysis, yet such poems may
depend upon our attempts to follow their metaphoric
threads. For us to understand such a poem, to feel it,
we must start our thoughts along the lines indicated by
the metaphors. Consider Shakespeare's sonnet 73 as an
example of this kind of poem:

That time of year thou may'st in me behold
When yellow leaves, or none, or few, do hang
Upon those boughs which shake against the cold—
Bare ruin'd choirs where late the sweet birds sang.
In me thou see'st the twilight of such day   5
As after Sunset fadeth in the West,
Which by and by black night doth take away,
Death's second self, that seals up all in rest.
In me thou see'st the glowing of such fire
That on the ashes of his youth doth lie,   10
As the death-bed whereon it must expire,
Consumed with that which it was nourish'd by.

This thou perceiv'st, which makes thy love more strong
To love that well which thou must leave ere long.

The images of the first twelve lines are all elabora-
tions of the simple notion that the speaker is getting
old. The last two lines are a dramatic assertion, also
rather simple. The speaker tells his listener that the
listener will love him all the more precisely because old
age and death threaten their relationship. We can infer
that the speaker is older than the listener, and in terms
of the dramatic situation we are entitled to wonder
whether these self-assured words are merely wishful
thinking, or an appraisal of the listener's attitude. How
does the imagery of the first twelve lines contribute to
the situation and to our understanding of it? We have
in these lines three separate but related metaphors,
each developed for four lines. The speaker says, in
effect, "You see in me—autumn; you see in me—twilight; you see in me——embers." These three metaphors for aging have in common certain qualities: a
growing coldness and darkness; suggestions of finality
and impending extinction. But each image generates its
own attitude and emphasizes a different aspect of the
aging process. The first four lines suggest an analogy
between an aging person and trees whose leaves have
fallen, leaving them exposed to cold winds. And the
bare trees suggest, by a further reach of metaphor, a
ruined and desolate church. Above all, this complex
metaphor generates sympathy for the speaker, a sym-

pathy based on our concern for lost beauty, for destruction of spiritual things, and for victims of the forces of
nature.

The next four lines, focusing on the twilight after
sunset, emphasize the threat of coming darkness. By
another extension of metaphor, "black night" is called
"Death's second self." The brevity of the time between
sunset and night increases our sense of sympathetic
urgency, and the introduction of "Death" takes us full
circle through the metaphors back to their object, an
aging man. The next four lines also introduce a complex metaphor. The speaker compares himself to the
glowing embers of a dying fire which lies upon "the
ashes of his youth." The fire becomes human, here, and
returns us again to the life of the speaker. This image
is the most intense of the three, because it likens the
arrival of age not merely to a seasonal change, worked
by the passage of time, but to the consumption or destruction of matter which can never be restored to its
original state. The ashes of the fire lying upon its death-
bed are forcible reminders that the speaker's body will
soon lie upon a death-bed, and will become ashes, to
be returned to the ashes and dust of the grave. It is the
emotional force of all "This" which the speaker main-
tains in the next-to-last line that the listener must perceive. And the confidence of the assertion is partly the
confidence of a poet who still has his poetical power.
He can still sing like a sweet bird and move his hearer
with his poetry. The imagery justifies the dramatic

situation, and the situation intensifies the significance of the imagery.

The Conceit. It is useful to think of the conceit as an extension of the simile in which aspects of the basic analogy are developed with a kind of relentless ingenuity. The "metaphysical" poets of the late sixteenth and the seventeenth century specialized in witty conceits. Here, for example, John Donne combines a dramatic situation with development of a conceit so that the images become an argument persuading his lady listener to give in.

THE FLEA

Marke but this flea, and marke in this,
How little that which thou deny'st me is;
It suck'd me first, and now sucks thee,
And in this flea, our two bloods mingled bee;
Thou know'st that this cannot be said
A sinne, nor shame, nor losse of maidenhead,
   Yet this enjoyes before it wooe,
    And pamper'd swells with one blood made of two,
    And this, alas, is more than wee would doe.

Oh stay, three lives in one flea spare,
Where wee almost, yea more than maryed are.
This flea is you and I, and this
Our mariage bed, and mariage temple is;
Though parents grudge, and you, w'are met,

And cloysterd in these living walls of Jet.
   Though use make you apt to kill mee,
   Let not to that, selfe murder added bee,
   And sacrilege, three sinnes in killing three.

Cruell and sodaine, hast thou since
Purpled thy naile, in blood of innocence?
Where could this flea guilty bee,
Except in that drop which it suckt from thee?
Yet thou triumph'st, and saist that thou
Find'st not thy selfe, nor mee the weaker now;
   'Tis true, then learne how false, feares bee;
   Just so much honor, when thou yeeld'st to mee,
   Will wast, as this flea's death tooke life from thee.

In the first two lines the speaker makes the basic analogy between the flea's having bitten both himself and the lady, and the act of love-making to which he would like to persuade her. In the rest of the poem he develops the analogy as an argument in a changing dramatic context. At the start of stanza two, the lady has threatened to swat the flea. By stanza three she has done so. And meanwhile the speaker has imaginatively transformed the flea into a marriage bed, a temple, a cloister, and a figure of the Holy Trinity (three in one); so that the flea's destruction can be hyperbolically described as murder, suicide, and sacrilege. All in preparation for the turn of the argument in the last three lines of the poem. Donne's conceit is both ingenious and playful in this poem. It is witty in more than one sense.

The Symbol. The symbol can be seen as an extension of the metaphor. In it, instead of saying that A is B-ish, or calling an A a B, the poet presents us with one half of the analogy only, and requires us to supply the missing part. In the long passage from Wordsworth's *Prelude* the poet first presented us with a description and then provided his own interpretation of it. The natural scene viewed from Snowdon was a symbol which Wordsworth turned back into a kind of metaphor by his interpretive meditation. Often, however, a poet will not provide an interpretation but will leave the reader to do the interpretive labor. This invites the reader to be creative and imaginative in a situation controlled by the poet. Bob Dylan's "Hard Rain" is a symbolic poem. And here is a symbolic poem by W. B. Yeats:*

THE DOLLS

A doll in the doll-maker's house
Looks at the cradle and bawls:
'That is an insult to us.'
But the oldest of all the dolls,
Who had seen, being kept for show,

* From *Collected Poems of William Butler Yeats.* Copyright 1916 by the Macmillan Co.; renewed 1944 by Bertha Georgie Yeats. Reprinted by permission of The Macmillan Co., Mr. M. B. Yeats, and Macmillan & Co., Ltd.

Generations of his sort,
Out-screams the whole shelf: 'Although
There's not a man can report
Evil of this place,
The man and the woman bring
Hither, to our disgrace,
A noisy and filthy thing.'
Hearing him groan and stretch
The doll-maker's wife is aware
Her husband has heard the wretch,
And crouched by the arm of his chair,
She murmurs into his ear,
Head upon shoulder leant:
'My dear, my dear, O dear,
It was an accident.'

This whole incident stands in a metaphoric relationship to something else. In other words, the poem is
only apparently about dolls and doll-makers. It is really
about something symbolized by the incident narrated.
What? And how do we go about determining what?
We must work very carefully from the situation toward possible analogies in the world of ideas and experience, first exploring the situation and images in
the poem. The situation derives from the doll-maker's
unique role as creator of two kinds of small, man-
shaped objects: dolls and children. The dolls in their
lifeless perfection resent the noise and filth produced
by an actual human child. The human baby is, in fact,

as the doll-maker's wife apologetically points out, not "made" in the same sense as dolls are made. Birth is an "accident"; dolls are deliberately constructed. The situation leads us outward until we see it as an illustration of the opposition between art and life, between the ideal and the real. The doll-maker himself thus symbolizes any artist who is obliged to live in the real world but create idealized objects, or any person who faces the impossible problem of realizing his ideas— or idealizing reality. Having got this far from the concrete situation of the poem, the reader is in a position to return and consider the ways in which Yeats has used language to control his tone and charge the scene with emotion. How should we react to the various characters in this little drama? What, finally, should our attitude be toward the real/ideal conflict which the drama illustrates?

The Pun. Often subjected to abuse as a "low" form of wit, the pun is essentially a kind of metaphor which can be used lightly and facetiously or for more serious purposes. Consider first some verses by Thomas Hood (selected by William Empson to exemplify punning techniques):

> For an eel I have learnt how to try
> By a method of Walton's own showing,
> > But a fisherman feels
> > Little prospect of eels
> On a path that's devoted to towing.

The pun on heel and toe *is* amusing (though one must drop the *h* from 'eel in Cockney style to make it work); but the pun—and the entire verse for that matter—is inconsequential. In another poem we can find Hood using a similar punning technique for more serious considerations:

> How frail is our uncertain breath!
> The laundress seems full hale, but death
> Shall her 'last linen' bring;
> The groom will die, like all his kind;
> And even the stable boy will find
> This life no stable thing. . . .
>
> Cook, butler, Susan, Jonathan,
> The girl that scours the pot and pan
> And those that tend the steeds,
> All, all shall have another sort
> Of service after this—in short
> The one the parson reads.

These puns on "stable" and "service" are playful but not funny. They use the basic device of the pun—dissimilar meanings for the same "word" or rather the same sound—to convey an attitude toward an idea. That both the life of a servant and his funeral are somehow included in that one piece of language—"service"—brings home to us the interconnection of life and death—which is the point of the poem.

Shakespeare was a master of the pun as of other metaphorical devices. Hamlet's bitter, punning responses to his uncle's smooth speeches are deadly serious and powerfully dramatic in their witty compression of his resentment.

> KING. . . . But now, my cousin Hamlet, and my son—
>
> HAMLET. [*Aside*]   A little more than kin and less than kind!
>
> KING.   How is it that the clouds still hang on you?
>
> HAMLET.   Not so, my lord.   I am too much i' the sun.

Hamlet and the King are more than *kin* (twice related: uncle/nephew and stepfather/son) but Hamlet feels they are not kindred spirits, not the same *kind*. And being called *son* by his father's murderer rouses all Hamlet's bitterness, causing him to return the King's metaphorical question about Hamlet's emotional weather with a pun that brings the metaphor back to the literal with a sarcastic bite: I am too much in the *son*.

THE LANGUAGE OF ANIMATION AND PERSONIFICATION

In addition to their playful or ingenious aspects, the various metaphorical devices help to generate the qualities of compression and intensity that we value in much poetry. Similar qualities are often achieved by other means, such as animation and personification.

Animation. Animation confers on objects or creatures a greater degree of awareness or purposefulness
than we normally credit them with. When Wordsworth
writes, "A hundred hills their dusky backs upheaved,"
he is presenting hills as if they were as alive as whales
or dolphins. This process is partly metaphorical. In its
context (see pp. 28–9) the animation of the hills is echoed
by that of the ocean ("his majesty"), the moon (*"Who,*
from *her sovereign* elevation, *gazed"*), and the torrents
(*"roaring* with one *voice"*).

Less romantic scenes can also be intensified by animation. Consider these lines from Johnson's "Vanity
of Human Wishes," which describe the treatment ac-
corded the portraits of a statesman whose power has
waned. Those who were honored to gaze at his features, now that no more is to be gained from the man,
suddenly find the likeness ugly:

> From every room descends the painted face,
> That hung the bright palladium of the place;
> And, smoked in kitchens, or in auctions sold,
> To better features yields the frame of gold;
> For now no more we trace in every line
> Heroic worth, benevolence divine;
> The form distorted justifies the fall,
> And detestation rids th' indignant wall.

In that last line Johnson intensifies his satire by ani-
mating the very wall on which the picture hangs—it,

even is indignant and wishes to be rid of these odious features. The removal itself is effected by a person who has dwindled into an attitude—"detestation."

Personification. In this example from Dr. Johnson, we have a kind of reverse personification—as a human being becomes an abstract idea. Personification usually works the other way, clothing abstractions with the attributes of personality. Of all the ideas presented as sentient beings, Love has been most frequently selected. In mythology, Love figures as the boy-god Cupid or Eros, offering poets a ready-made personification which they have often used. The mechanical use of traditional personification can be a dull and dreary thing. But observe Sir Philip Sidney as he personifies Love in this sonnet, and finds ways to make concrete a whole range of other abstractions such as reverence, fear, hope, will, memory, and desire. If Love is personified here, these other notions are objectified—turned into material objects.

> I on my horse, and Love on me doth try
>> Our horsemanships, while by strange work I prove
>> A horseman to my horse, a horse to Love;
>> And now man's wrongs in me, poor beast, descry.
>
> The reins wherewith my rider doth me tie,
>> Are humbled thoughts, which bit of reverence move,
>> Curb'd in with fear, but with gilt boss above
>> Of hope, which makes it seem fair to the eye.

> The wand is will; thou, fancy, saddle art,
>> Girt fast by memory, and while I spur
>> My horse, he spurs with sharp desire my heart:
>
> He sits me fast, however I do stir:
>> And now hath made me to his hand so right,
>> That in the manage my self takes delight.

The dominant image of Love as horseman provides the subordinate imagery for making concrete the other abstractions which serve to amplify this picture of a love-ridden man. The effectiveness of the poem depends on the ingenuity with which the poet has matched the objects and ideas to one another, relating all to the dominant personification of Love. Like Spenser's epic simile, Sidney's personification seems to breed subordinate metaphors easily, gracefully, and naturally.

THE ANTI-METAPHORICAL LANGUAGE OF IRONY

Verbal irony may be said to start with simple negation of resemblance in situations where resemblance is customarily insisted upon: as in Shakespeare's sonnet 130, which begins,

> My mistress' eyes are nothing like the sun;
> Coral is far more red than her lips red:
> If snow be white, why then her breasts are dun;
> If hairs be wires, black wires grow on her head.

The anti-similes of the first three lines serve the same function as the ugly metaphor in line 4. All four lines present attacks on what the speaker will name in the last line as "false compare"—the misuse by poets of the metaphorical dimension of poetical language.

Usually, however, irony is not so straightforward. In fact, we normally think of it as involving some indirection or misleading of the reader—some gap between what the words *seem* to be saying and what they *are* saying. Thus, in this Shakespearean sonnet, after eight more lines of plain speaking about an ordinary human female, the speaker concludes,

> And yet, by heaven, I think my love as rare
> As any She belied by false compare.

What we might have taken as disparagement of the lady turns out to be praise after all. She is not uglier than the others; she just has a lover who won't exaggerate her beauty with the usual clichés. Thus, there is an irony in the disparity between the apparent disparagement of the lady in the first part of the poem and the praise of her at the end. We can see, then, in those opening lines, a kind of understatement, which works finally to convince us of the lady's beauty more effectively than a conventionally exaggerated simile of "false compare" would have done.

Understatement and overstatement are two of the most frequently used kinds of verbal irony. When Swift causes a character to observe (in prose), "Last

Week I saw a Woman *flay'd,* and you will hardly be-
lieve, how much it altered her Person for the worse"—
the main thing that strikes us is the awful inadequacy
of the sentiment for the event. Disparity, contrast, incongruity—these things are at the heart of verbal
irony. And, perhaps at the heart of that heart lies the
notion that all words are inadequate for the representation of things. The poet as maker of metaphors may
be seen as a genuine magician, bringing new things
into the world, or as a charlatan pretending with feeble
words to unite things which are essentially separate.
Metaphor emphasizes the creative dimension of language, irony its tricky dimension.

For example, in Marvell's "To his Coy Mistress" the
exaggerated protestations of the extent that the speaker's love would require "Had we but world enough and
time" are all based on the view that of course we do
not have world enough and time. Even before we get
there, we sense the presence of the "But" on which the
poem will make its turn:

> But at my back I always hear
> Time's winged chariot hurrying near;

The contrast between what the speaker *would* do:

> Two hundred years should go to praise
> Thine eyes, and on thy forehead gaze:
> Two hundred to adore each breast:
> And thirty thousand to the rest;

and what he *does* urge:

> Now let us sport us while we may,

is an ironic one, enhanced by the extreme distance in time between hundreds or thousands of years and "Now."

Irony can also take the form of metaphorical over-statement, as it does in Alexander Pope's description of coffee being poured into a China cup:

> From silver spouts the grateful liquors glide,
> While China's earth receives the smoking tide.

These lines are metaphorical in that they present one thing (pouring a cup of coffee) in terms of another image (a kind of burning flood pouring over the main-land of China); but they are ironic in that the equa-tion is made mainly so that we will perceive the disparity between the two images and enjoy their *in-*congruity. Something of this reverse anti-metaphorical wit is present in many metaphors. John Donne's "The Flea" has a witty, ironic dimension derived from the inappropriateness of his basic image. To call a flea a temple is to establish a very far-fetched metaphor. The conceits used by Donne and other "metaphysical" poets of his time often have an ironic dimension. Samuel Johnson characterized the metaphysical poets precisely in terms of this dimension—a special and extreme form of "wit" based on the "discovery of occult resemblances in things apparently unlike," and resulting in poems in which "the most heterogeneous ideas are yoked by violence together." Johnson's description emphasizes ("yoked by violence") the tension between metaphoric comparison and ironic contrast in many metaphysical conceits. Conceits tend to be witty, cerebral, unnatural; while metaphors are serious, imaginative, and natural. The metaphors of Romantic poetry (as in the lines from *The Prelude*) are perceptions of relationships felt actually to exist. Metaphysical conceits often establish powerful but artificial relationships where one would least expect to find them.

Linking incongruous things is a feature of most kinds of witty poetry. A simple list with one incongruous element can serve to indict a whole way of life, as when Alexander Pope surveys the debris on a lady's dressing table:

Puffs, Powders, Patches, Bibles, Billet-doux

The inclusion of Bibles among love letters and cosmetics suggests a confusion between worldly and spiritual values—a failure to distinguish between true and false worth. The list is funny, but in an ironic and satiric way—as is this list of possible calamities from the same poem:

Whether the nymph shall break Diana's law,
Or some frail China jar receive a flaw;
Or stain her honour or her new brocade;

Forget her prayers or miss a masquerade;
Or lose her heart or necklace at a ball;

Here Pope mixes several serious matters of the spirit with trivial and worldly items. The breaking of Diana's law of chastity is equated with damage to a jar. A single verb, "stain," governs two objects—"honour" and "brocade"—of different qualities and intensities. By this manipulation of grammar Pope makes us forcibly aware of the frivolousness of an attitude toward life which equates things that properly should have different values. He brings those two objects under that one verb so that we will feel a powerful urge to part them in our minds, resolving the incongruity by separating the elements he has brought together.

Another kind of incongruity is that achieved by Byron in such passages as this one, which presents a romantic lover trying to keep his mind on his beloved while his stomach is attacked by seasickness:

"Sooner shall heaven kiss earth—(here he fell sicker)
    Oh, Julia! what is every other woe?—
(For God's sake let me have a glass of liquor;
    Pedro, Battista, help me down below.)
Julia my love—(you rascal, Pedro, quicker)—
    Oh, Julia—(this curst vessel pitches so)—
Beloved Julia, hear me still beseeching!"
(Here he grew inarticulate with retching.)

The irony here is more a matter of drama than of language; but the difference between the language of the speaker's romantic assertions and his cries to his servants, supports the dramatic irony. The narrator points up the contrast by mis-rhyming "retching" with "beseeching" in the last two lines.

BEYOND METAPHOR AND IRONY

Much of the best contemporary poetry presents combinations of images and ideas so stretched and disconnected that they go beyond metaphor and yet so serious and appropriate they transcend irony also. The difficulty in understanding many modern poems stems from a profusion of images that seem ironically disconnected, but nevertheless suggest genuine metaphorical connection. We can find a relatively simple illustration in a few lines from a ballad by W. H. Auden:*

> The glacier knocks in the cupboard,
>   The desert sighs in the bed
> And the crack in the tea-cup opens
>   A lane to the land of the dead.

Here Auden seems to be operating with ironic incongruities—the glacier in the cupboard and so on—but this collection of incongruities adds up to a quite coherent statement about the absurd and empty horror that threatens much of modern life. Such a collection of images seems to combine qualities of conceit and symbol with ironic incongruity, leaving us to resolve the problem of whether these assertions are ironic overstatements or powerful metaphors for our condition.

A poem composed of a number of these high-tension ironic metaphors can be immediately intelligible in a general way and still difficult to reduce to prose sense at every point. But we should make the effort to establish prose sense—or possible prose senses—for each image and situation in such a poem, because even if we do not succeed entirely, we will be testing the ultimate intelligibility of the poem, the durability of its interest. As with certain kinds of modern art, it is sometimes hard to separate the fraudulent from the real in contemporary poetry. If we cannot discover intelligibility and coherence in a poem, if its images and situations do not enhance one another, we are confronted by either a fraudulent poem or a poem which is beyond us—one which we have not as yet learned how to read. Differences in poetic quality cannot be demonstrated conclusively, yet they exist. The following poem by a young American poet is offered as a problem in intelligibility and evaluation. Does it make sense? Does it work? Is it good?*

SURVIVAL OF THE FITTEST GROCERIES

The violence in the newspapers is pure genius
A daily gift to the reader
From some poet who wants to keep in good with us
Brown-noser wastepaperbasket-emptier

I shot 437 people that day
2 were still alive when I killed them
Why do people want to be exhumed movie-stars
I mean rats still biting them, the flesh of comets, why do they
    walk around like that?

I'm going to throw all of you into the refrigerator
And leave you to claw it out with the vegetables and meats

* From "Survival of the Fittest Groceries," by William Knott (Saint Geraud). Reprinted from *The Young American Poets*, edited by Paul Carroll. Copyright © 1968 by Follett Publishing Co. and used by their permission.

PART FOUR

MUSIC

The musical element in poetry is the hardest to talk about because it is non-verbal. Our responses to rhythm and to pleasing combinations of sounds are in a sense too immediate, too fundamental to be comprehended in words. Yet music is important in all poetry, and for most poetry written before the last half-century it is crucial. Therefore, we must try to get some sort of verbal grasp of this poetical element, simply in order to do justice to most poetic achievement. Students generally prefer discussing one aspect of poetry to another in an order something like this:

1. ideas
2. situations
3. language
4. metrics

But if we are concerned about what makes poetry poetry rather than some other kind of composition, we should probably reverse this order. If a piece of writing is neither especially rhythmical nor especially ironic or metaphorical in its language, it is not poetry, regardless of its dramatic situations or the ideas it presents.

In my experience, students are not only least interested in metrics of all the elements of poetry; they are also least competent in it. To demonstrate this one need only ask them to translate a few sentences of prose into a simple, versified equivalent. Most will find this very difficult to do. No wonder they don't like poetry. They can't hear it properly. Fortunately, the fundamentals of versification are teachable to some extent, and should be part of any poetical curriculum. In the pages that follow, these fundamentals are presented in a fairly simple way, with a minimum of special terminology.

METRICS

Metrics has to do with all rhythmical effects in poetry. In English versification this means that it is largely a matter of accents and pauses. The pauses are determined by the usual grammatical principles that govern our speech and writing, and are indicated by the usual grammatical symbols: periods, commas, and so on. But one new factor is added. The end of a line of verse is

itself a mark of punctuation. If a line ends with a regular mark of punctuation we call it end-stopped. If the
last word of a line is followed by no punctuation and
is part of a continuing grammatical unit like a pre-
positional phrase, we call the line run-on, or enjambed.
In end-stopped lines the line-end works *with* the
punctuation and reinforces it, making each line a tight
unit of thought. In enjambed lines the line-end works
against the punctuation, throwing certain words into
a prominence that they would not ordinarily have. The
enjambed line really adds a special kind of poetical
punctuation to the language: something which is at
once more and less than a comma. Poets who use free
verse forms with no regular rhythm are very de-
pendent on enjambment to give their words a special
poetical quality. Reconsider the little poem by Williams:

> so much depends
> upon
>
> a red wheel
> barrow
>
> glazed with rain
> water
>
> beside the white
> chickens.

If we write this out as prose we get

So much depends upon a red wheelbarrow, glazed
with rainwater, beside the white chickens.

This is a simple, declarative prose sentence, with a
couple of adjectival phrases tacked on, set off with
commas. Has anything been lost by this rearrange-
ment of the poem on the page? I should say decidedly
so. The assertion being made is much less convincing
in plain prose. The free-verse form of the sentence
uses its line-endings to work against the prose movement, slowing it up, and providing a metrical equivalent for the visual highlighting of the images. Just
where we would bring the words closest together in
prose—making single words out of "wheel" and "bar-
row," "rain" and "water"—Williams has pulled them
apart by breaking the line in mid-word. The poem may
or may not carry us to final agreement with its assertion, but the free-verse form of it certainly convinces
us of the speaker's earnestness. We get a sense of how
much *he* cares about what he is saying from the care
with which he has spaced out his words. And when
we read the poem aloud, with little pauses at line-ends,
it carries us further toward conviction than the same
sentence in its prosaic form.

That is a simple illustration of how poetry's special
line-end punctuation can group words in a rhythm
different from the rhythm of normal speech or prose.

Here is a further illustration of how a poet can use the line-end to achieve an ironic effect virtually unduplicatable in prose. E. E. Cummings begins a poem this way:*

> pity this busy monster, manunkind,
> not.

The first word of the second line absolutely reverses the meaning of the first line. We pause, with a comma, at the end of line 1. We stop entirely, with a period, after the first word of line 2. We hover, thus, with the wrong meaning until we are given the word which changes it, whereupon we stop to contemplate the admonition offered us in the whole opening sentence. Consider it rearranged as plain prose:

> Pity this busy monster, manunkind, not.

or more prosaically,

> Do not pity this busy monster, manunkind.

or still more prosaically,

> Do not pity this busy, unkind monster, man.

By unraveling the poetical arrangement and combination of the words, we have destroyed the force of the

* From "Pity this busy monster man unkind," by E. E. Cummings, in *Poems 1923–1954*. Reprinted by permission of Harcourt, Brace and World, Inc. and MacGibbon and Kee.

admonition, taking away its suspense and eliminating the recoil in the original last word. In verse which is not markedly rhythmical, unusual pauses and arrangements of words are the principal metrical device.

In verse which is regularly rhythmical, however, the rhythm or meter itself is the crucial metrical element. Poetical arrangement does something to prosaic language, but not as much as rhythm, which lifts an utterance and moves it in the direction of music. Just as the line-end pauses in a poem can work with or against the normal grammatical pauses of speech and prose, poetic rhythm can work both with and against our normal patterns of pronunciation. In speech we begin with standard grammatical pronunciations for words. Take the word "defense." Normally we pronounce this word by accenting the first syllable lightly and the second syllable heavily. Indicating light accent by ∪ and heavy accent by —, we pronounce the word this way: defḗnse. That is grammatical accent or grammatical stress. But in certain situations we might change this pronunciation for purposes of emphasis, as in, "It's not *off*ense that's important, it's *def*ense." Here we pronounce the word défense. This is not grammatical stress but rhetorical stress. We have altered the usual pattern of light and heavy accent in order to make a point. (Grammar, of course, keeps changing, and the repeated use of one particular rhetorical pattern can eventually alter standard pro-

nunciation. Broadcasts of football and basketball
games, for instance, are helping to make defense the
$$- \smile$$
standard way to say the word.)

Both grammatical and rhetorical stress operate in
poetry, where they are complicated by a third kind
of accent, which we may call poetical stress. Poetical
stress is a regular system of accents which establishes
the basic rhythm of a poem. There are only two fundamental systems of poetic stress in English verse,
though there are many variations on them. Most frequently, English verse simply alternates light and
heavy accents, giving every other syllable the same
stress. Like this:

$$\smile \quad - \quad \smile - \quad \smile \quad - \quad \smile - \quad \smile \quad -$$
The woods decay, the woods decay and fall

Less frequently, English verse uses two light syllables
between each heavy stress. Like this:

$$\smile \quad \smile - \smile \quad \smile \quad - \quad \smile \quad \smile \quad - \quad \smile \quad \smile \quad -$$
The Assyrian came down like the wolf on the fold
$$\smile \quad \smile \quad - \smile \quad \smile \quad - \quad \smile \quad \smile - \smile \quad \smile \quad -$$
And his cohorts were gleaming in purple and gold

The rhythm of this second metrical pattern is more
insistent than that of the first. The simple da-dum,
da-dum of "The woods decay" is more like the spoken
language than the da-da-dum, da-da-dum of "like the
wolf on the fold."

When talking about metrics it is useful to have a

term for the units which are repeated to make the pattern. It is customary to call these units "feet." In the first example above, we have five repeated units in the line, five feet, divided this way:

$$\breve{} \quad - \qquad \breve{} \quad - \quad \breve{} \qquad - \qquad \breve{} \quad - \qquad \breve{} \quad -$$
The woods | decay, | the woods | decay | and fall

In the second example each line has four feet, divided like this:

$$\breve{} \quad \breve{} \quad - \qquad \breve{} \quad \breve{} \qquad - \qquad \breve{} \quad \breve{} \quad - \qquad \breve{} \quad \breve{} \quad -$$
And his co | horts were gleam | ing in pur | ple and gold

In describing metrical patterns we usually state the number of feet in the basic line and name the standard foot in each line. The traditional name for the foot used in the first example (da-dum) is the "iamb." The traditional name for the foot used in the second example (da-da-dum) is the "anapest." In referring to the number of feet in the basic line of a poem, it is customary to use numerical prefixes derived from the Greek. Thus,

one-foot line =	mono	+ meter =	monometer
two-foot line =	di	+ meter =	dimeter
three-foot line =	tri	+ meter =	trimeter
four-foot line =	tetra	+ meter =	tetrameter
five-foot line =	penta	+ meter =	pentameter
six-foot line =	hexa	+ meter =	hexameter

We could skip the Greek and talk about such things as "lines with ten syllables that go da-dum" and so on, but it is finally easier to learn the accepted terms and say simply "iambic pentameter."

The iamb and the anapest each have a variant foot which is made by placing the accented syllable at the beginning of each foot rather than at the end. These are called the trochee (dum-da) and the dactyl (dum-da-da). They are not used very consistently for one good reason. Rhyme in poetry is pleasing only if it includes the last accented syllable in a line *and all the unaccented syllables that follow it.* Thus, if I write,

$$\cup - \cup - \quad \cup \quad - \quad \cup -$$
Upon a mid | night drear | y once

I need find only a one-syllable rhyme for my rhyming line, such as:

Upon a midnight dreary once
I tried my hand at kicking punts

But if I use the trochee, and write

$$- \cup \quad - \cup \quad - \cup \quad - \cup$$
Once u | pon a | midnight | dreary

then I must rhyme

Once upon a midnight dreary
Of kicking punts my foot was weary.

The trochaic foot can, in fact, grow quite wearisome if carried through to the rhyme word consistently; so we often get a variation that looks like this:

$$— \cup — \cup — \cup \quad —$$
Tiger, Tiger burning bright
$$— \cup \quad — \cup — \cup \quad —$$
In the forests of the night

These lines first appear trochaic (dum-da) and end by looking iambic (da-dum). (Though, actually the second line is more complicated in a way we will consider later on.) The two lines could be made fully iambic by a very slight change in each:

$$\cup \quad — \cup — \cup — \quad \cup \quad —$$
O, Tiger, Tiger burning bright
$$\cup — \quad \cup — \cup — \cup \quad —$$
Within the forest of the night

or we could make them fully trochaic by this kind of alteration:

$$— \cup \quad — \cup — \cup \quad — \cup$$
Tiger, Tiger burning brightly,
$$— \cup \quad — \quad \cup — \cup — \cup$$
Roaming through the forest nightly

In order to name the metrical pattern of "Tiger, Tiger" we must supply an imaginary unaccented syllable at one end of the line or the other, like this:

$$\cup — \quad \cup \quad — \quad \cup \quad — \quad \cup \quad —$$
x Ti | ger, Ti | ger, burn | ing bright

or this:

$$— \cup \quad — \cup \quad — \quad \cup \quad — \quad \cup$$
Tiger, | Tiger, | burning | bright x

These maneuverings strongly suggest that the special terminology of metrical analysis is not important in itself, and that beyond the major distinction between the two-syllable foot and the three-syllable foot, we need not be terribly fussy in classifying. What, then, is the use of all these special terms?

The art of metrics involves a poet's ability to generate and maintain a consistent meter without destroying normal patterns of grammar and syntax. To succeed metrically a poet must make language dance without making it unnatural. And a really crucial aspect of this art is perceptible only when we have the terminology to recognize it. Any absolutely regular meter quickly becomes boring through repetition. But a totally irregular poem is totally without the kind of interest and pleasure that rhythm provides. All good poets who work in regular meters introduce metrical variations into their poems. The simplest way to understand this is to see the variations as substitutions of a different sort of foot for the one called for by the established meter of the poem. (The second line of Blake's "Tiger, Tiger" is not quite the same as the first. Can you devise alternative ways to describe its

rhythm?) As an example of metrical variation, consider
this stanza from a poem by Housman:*

⌣ — ⌣ — ⌣ — ⌣
With rue my heart is laden
⌣ — ⌣ — ⌣ —
For golden friends I had
⌣ — ⌣ ⌣ — ⌣ — ⌣
For many a rose-lipt maiden
⌣ — ⌣ ⌣ — ⌣ —
And many a lightfoot lad.

The meter is basically iambic, complicated a little
by the extra syllable of a feminine rhyme in alternate
lines (laden, maiden—two-syllable rhymes are called
"feminine"). But the basic meter is varied by the addition of one anapestic foot in lines three and four. The
second (and last) stanza of that poem goes like this:

By brooks too broad for leaping
The lightfoot boys are laid;
The rose-lipt girls are sleeping
In fields where roses fade.

This looks almost absolutely regular—iambic trimeter
with alternate feminine rhyme—but it is not quite.

Both grammar and rhetoric urge us to accent and elongate the sound of the word "too" in the first line. Thus the line must be scanned (analyzed metrically) this way:

$$\breve{} \quad - \qquad - \quad - \qquad \breve{} \quad - \quad (\breve{})$$
by brooks | too broad | for leaping

The second foot of this line has two accented syllables and no unaccented one. This is a kind of foot that is often used as a substitute but never as the metrical basis for a whole poem. Its technical name is "spondee." Housman has used the spondee here for a slight variation of his rhythm—one which is almost unnoticeable to the analytic eye, but works subtly on the ear to prevent the rhythm from becoming monotonous.

Having noticed that substitution, we might notice also that in both stanzas the words "lightfoot" and "rose-lipt" work gently in a spondaic direction. In both stanzas these words appear so that the heavy accent of the iamb falls on their first syllable. But that second syllable is a word in its own right, and one which might well take a heavy accent in another metrical situation, such as this:

$$\breve{} \quad - \quad \breve{} \quad - \quad \breve{}$$
My foot is weary,
$$\breve{} \quad - \quad \breve{} \quad -\breve{}$$
My eye is teary,
$$\breve{} \quad - \quad \breve{} \quad -\breve{}$$
My lip is beery.

"Foot" and "lip" (or "lipt) can both take heavy accents. In Housman's stanzas the syllables "foot" and
"lipt," falling where we would expect light accents,
actually result in something between heavy and light.
The basic terminology of metrical analysis establishes
only the simple distinction between heavy and light,
thus it cannot take us too far into any metrical subtle-
ties. In scansion, however, we need to consider subtle-
ties, and should probably be ready to use at least one
more symbol to indicate a stress between heavy and
light. Using a combination of the two stress marks we
already have in operation to indicate an intermediate
stress, we might re-scan the first stanza this way:

∪   —   ∪   —   ∪ — ∪
With rue my heart is laden
∪   —   ∪   —   ∪ —
for golden friends I had,
∪ — ∪ ∪ —   ∪̆   — ∪
For many a rose-lipt maiden
∪   — ∪ ∪ —   ∪̆   —
And many a lightfoot lad.

Then we could point out that the intermediate accents
                   ∪̆   ∪̆
on lipt and foot make the last feet of lines 3 and 4
partially spondaic.

Thus far we have considered the metrics of this
little poem only in terms of its pleasing variation
within a firmly established pattern. We can see how
the pattern is established in the first two lines of the

first stanza, and then varied subtly in most of the succeeding lines, until the pattern reasserts itself in the perfectly regular last line. Now, we are in a position to deal with the question of the relationship of the metrics to the meaning of the poem. The poem makes a simple statement about sadness felt for the death of those who were once agile and pretty. But death is never mentioned. It is evoked metaphorically through words like "laid" and "sleeping." These metaphors are very gentle, suggesting more the peace of the grave than any decay or destruction. In the second stanza the speaker also suggests delicately the frustration and sadness felt by those in the world of the living. The unleapable brooks symbolize things unachievable in life; the fading roses symbolize the impermanence of living things. The peace of the dead is ironically contrasted with the sadness of the living. The speaker is finally rueful not just because his golden friends are dead but because *he* is alive.

How does the meter relate to all this? Iambic trimeter calls for a good deal of rhyme—a rhyming sound every third foot. The addition of feminine rhymes in alternate lines makes for even more rhyming syllables. If we compare this metrical situation with that in another poem about death and decay, we should notice something about the effect of meter.

Slow, slow, fresh fount, keep time with my salt tears;
   Yet slower, yet; O faintly gentle springs;

List to the heavy part the music bears,
　　Woe weeps out her division when she sings:
　　　　Droop herbs and flowers;
　　　　Fall grief in showers;
　　　　Our beauties are not ours.
　　　　　　O, I could still,
　　Like melting snow upon some craggy hill,
　　　　　Drop, drop, drop, drop,
　　Since nature's pride is now a withered daffodil.

How should this first line be scanned? Something like
this:

　— 　 — 　 | 　— 　 — 　 | 　◡ 　— 　 | 　◡ 　◡ 　 | 　— 　 —
Slow, slow, | fresh fount, | keep time | with my | salt tears;

Here we have that rarity, a line almost completely
spondaic—with only a suggestion of iambs in the
third and fourth feet. An iambic pattern establishes
itself gradually in the poem, but the verse is dominated
by spondees, even in the short lines:

　　　— 　　— 　◡ 　— (◡)
　　　Droop herbs and flowers;
　　　— 　　— 　◡ 　— (◡)
　　　Fall grief in showers;
　　　— 　　— 　◡ 　— 　— 　—(◡)
　　　Our beauties are not ours.

　　　　　(These rhyme words can all be scanned
　　　　　as either one or two syllables.)

In addition to this spondaic domination, the lines are frequently broken by pauses—those indicated by the punctuation, as well as those which naturally follow imperatives like "Droop" and "Fall." These pauses and the spondees work together to give the poem a slow, hesitant, funereal movement like the sound of muffled drums. This meter works in a metaphoric or harmonious relationship to the sense of the poem, which is a direct utterance of grief over seasonal decay and the death it symbolizes.

Now, how does this compare to the movement of the Housman poem? Housman's iambic trimeter, virtually pauseless except for line-ends, is a much lighter, almost gay meter. The stresses bounce regularly, the lines flow smoothly, the rhymes chime insistently. This pattern establishes an ironic or contrasting relationship to the mournful sense of the words, but is perfectly appropriate because the words themselves are finally ironic. Housman deals with death lightly, easily, if wryly. Jonson works hard to make us respond seriously and sadly. The frequent pauses, the heavy spondees, the varying length of the lines—all these work to reinforce the sadness and seriousness of Jonson's words. Both poems have a pronounced musical dimension, but Housman's is like a spritely ballad meter and Jonson's is like a funeral dirge.

Before considering rhyme and other sound effects further, we need to look at one last important dimension of metrics. The standard line of English verse which is meant to be spoken rather than sung is a line of five iambic feet—iambic pentameter. This is the basic line of Chaucer's *Canterbury Tales*, of Spenser's *Faerie Queene*, of Shakespeare's plays, of Milton's *Paradise Lost*, of the satires of Dryden and Pope, of Byron's *Don Juan*, of Wordsworth's *Prelude*, of Browning's *The Ring and the Book*. This line often appears unrhymed, as in Shakespeare's plays (for the most part), *Paradise Lost*, and *The Prelude*; or in pairs of rhymed lines. Technically, the unrhymed iambic pentameter line is called blank verse; the paired rhymes are called couplets. In both these iambic pentameter lines, an important element is the mid-line pause or "caesura." Varying the location of the caesura is an important way of preventing monotony in blank verse and pentameter couplets. Consider, for example, these lines from Milton:

High on a Throne of Royal State, which far
Outshone the wealth of *Ormus* and of *Ind*,
Or where the gorgeous East with richest hand
Show'rs on her Kings *Barbaric* Pearl and Gold,
Satan exalted sat, by merit rais'd   5
To that bad eminence; and from despair
Thus high uplifted beyond hope, aspires
Beyond thus high, insatiate to pursue
Vain War with Heav'n, and by success untaught
His proud imaginations thus display'd.   10

If we locate the obvious caesurae—those indicated by internal punctuation marks—we find this situation:

line 1 . . . end of 4th foot
line 2 . . . none
line 3 . . . none
line 4 . . . none
line 5 . . . end of 3rd foot
line 6 . . . end of 3rd foot
line 7 . . . end of 4th foot
line 8 . . . end of 2nd foot
line 9 . . . end of 2nd foot
line 10 . . . none

In reading the poem aloud, we will find ourselves pausing slightly, at some point in nearly every line, whether a pause is indicated by punctuation or not. Thus, we can mark the whole passage this way, using a single slash for a slight pause and two for a notice-able one, three for a full stop.

High on a throne of Royal State,// which far
Outshone/ the wealth of *Ormus*/ and of *Ind*,
Or where the gorgeous East/ with richest hand
Show'rs on her kings/ *Barbaric* Pearl and Gold,
Satan exalted sat,// by merit rais'd
To that bad eminence;/// and from despair
Thus high uplifted beyond hope,// aspires
Beyond thus high,// insatiate to pursue

Vain war with Heav'n,// and by success untaught
His proud imaginations/ thus display'd.

By varying end-stopped lines with enjambed, and de-
ploying caesurae of varying strengths at different
points in his line, Milton continually shifts his pauses
to prevent the march of his lines from growing wearisome. He also uses substitute feet frequently—especially a trochee or spondee in the first foot of a line. I
count three trochees and one spondee in the first feet
of these ten lines. Check this count yourself.

Now consider Alexander Pope's use of enjambment,
caesura, and substitution of feet in the following lines.
Pope uses a tight form, with punctuation coming
nearly always at the end of each couplet. These closed
couplets (as opposed to enjambed or open couplets) in
iambic pentameter are called "heroic" couplets because
they were the standard verse form of Restoration
heroic drama, (but they might better be called satiric,
because they have been most successful in the satiric
poems of Dryden, Pope, and Samuel Johnson.) In such
a tight form as the heroic couplet, great skill is needed
to avoid monotony. When we read only the real mas-
ters of such a form, we tend to take such skill for
granted, but it is far from easy. Here we find Pope
talking about poetic blunders and poetic skill, modu-
lating his own verse deftly to illustrate the points he
is making. (The "Alexandrine" referred to is an iambic hexameter line, occasionally used for variety in

English iambic pentameter forms.) These two passages from Pope's "Essay on Criticism" are printed here widely spaced, to allow the student to write in his own scansion.

These equal syllables alone require,

Though oft the ear the open vowels tire;

While expletives their feeble aid do join;

And ten low words oft creep in one dull line:

While they ring round the same unvaried chimes,

With sure returns of still expected rhymes;

Where'er you find "the cooling western breeze,"

In the next line, it "whispers through the trees: "

If crystal streams "with pleasing murmurs creep,"

The reader's threatened (not in vain) with "sleep: "

Then, at the last and only couplet fraught

With some unmeaning thing they call a thought,

A needless Alexandrine ends the song

That, like a wounded snake, drags its slow length along.

True ease in writing comes from art, not chance,

As those move easiest who have learned to dance.

'Tis not enough no harshness gives offence,

The sound must seem an Echo to the sense:

Soft is the strain when Zephyr gently blows,

And the smooth stream in smoother numbers flows;

But when loud surges lash the sounding shore,

The hoarse, rough verse should like the torrent roar:

When Ajax strives some rock's vast weight to throw,

The line too labours, and the words move slow;

Not so, when swift Camilla scours the plain,

Flies o'er th' unbending corn, and skims along the main.

Rhyme is an important element in musical poetry, but much less so in dramatic poetry—where it can be too artificial—or in meditative poetry. Associated with rhyme as elements designed to generate a pleasure in sound which is almost purely esthetic are such devices as alliteration and assonance. Alliteration is the repetition of the same sound at the beginning of words in the same line or adjacent lines. Assonance is the repetition of vowel sounds in the same or adjacent lines. For full rhyme we require the same vowel sounds which end in the same consonantal sounds. "Fight" and "foot" are alliterative. "Fight" and "bike" are assonant. "Fight" and "fire" are both assonant and alliterative but do not make a rhyme. "Fight" and "bite" make a rhyme. Consider the metrical and sonic effects in this stanza of a poem by Swinburne:

Till the slow sea rise and the sheer cliff crumble,
 Till terrace and meadow the deep gulfs drink,
Till the strength of the waves of the high tides humble
 The fields that lessen, the rocks that shrink,
Here now in his triumph where all things falter,
 Stretched out on the spoils that his own hand spread,
As a god self-slain on his own strange altar,
  Death lies dead.

The meter is mainly a mixture of anapests and spondees—an exotic combination of rapid and slow feet. Can you discern any particular pattern in the way the feet are combined? Is there variation in the pattern? What do rhyme, assonance, and alliteration contribute to the pattern?

In addition to its purely esthetic or decorative effect, designed to charm the reader out of a critical posture and into a receptive one, rhyme can be used for just the opposite effect. In satiric or comic verse, strained rhymes are often used to awaken the reader's wits and give him a comic kind of pleasure. Ogden Nash often combines strained rhymes with lines of awkwardly unequal length for especially absurd effects. But something similar can be achieved within fairly strict formal limits. In the following stanza from Byron's *Don*

Juan, we find the poet using feminine and even triple rhyme with deliberate clumsiness:

> Tis pity learned virgins ever wed
>   With persons of no sort of education,
> Or gentlemen, who, though well born and bred,
>   Grow tired of scientific conversation:
> I don't choose to say much upon this head,
>   I'm a plain man, and in a single station,
> But—Oh! ye lords of ladies intellectual,
> Inform us truly, have they not hen-peck'd you all?

The last rhyme in particular is surprising, audacious, and deliberately strained—echoing in this way the sense of the stanza. Like imagery and metrics, rhyme can be used harmoniously or ironically, to establish or to break a mood.

PART FIVE

APPROACHING A POEM

We don't, if we are honest, keep in readiness a number of different approaches to poems or to people. We try to keep our integrity. But at the same time we must recognize and accept the otherness that we face. In getting to know a person or a poem we make the kind of accommodation that I have called tact. But we do not pretend, we do not emote falsely, and we try not to make stock responses to surface qualities. We do not judge a man by his clothes or even by his skin. We do not judge a poem by words or ideas taken out of their full poetic context. We do not consider a statement in a poem without attention to its dramatic context, the overtones generated by its metaphors and ironies, the mood established by its metrics. And we try to give each element of every poem its proper weight.

Obviously, there can be no single method for treating every poem with tact. What is required is a flexible procedure through which we can begin to understand the nature of any poem. The suggestions which follow are intended to facilitate such a procedure. Like everything else in this book they should serve as a scaffolding only—a temporary structure inside of which the real building takes shape. Like any scaffolding, this one must be discarded as soon as it becomes constricting or loses its usefulness. Like good manners learned by rote, this procedure will never amount to anything until it is replaced by naturally tactful behavior. Then it will have served its purpose.

1. Try to grasp the expressive dimension of the poem first. This means especially getting a clear sense of the nature and situation of the speaker. What are the circumstances under which he says, writes, or thinks these words? Who hears them? Are they part of an ongoing action which is implied by them?

2. Consider the relative importance of the narrative-dramatic dimension and the descriptive-meditative dimension in the poem. Is the main interest psychological or philosophical—in character or in idea? Or is the poem's verbal playfulness or music its main reason for being? How do the nature of the speaker and the situation in which he speaks color the ideas and attitudes presented?

3. After you have a sense of the poem's larger, expressive dimension, re-read it with particular attention

to the play of language. Consider the way that metaphor and irony color the ideas and situations. How does the language work to characterize the speaker or to color the ideas presented with shadings of attitude? How important is sheer word-play or verbal wit in the poem? How well do the images and ideas fit together and reinforce one another in a metaphoric or ironic way?

4. Re-read the poem yet again with special attention to its musical dimension. To the extent that it seems important, analyze the relation of rhythm and rhyme to the expressive dimension of the poem.

5. Throughout this process, reading the poem aloud can be helpful in establishing emphases and locating problems. Parts of a poem which are not fully understood will prove troublesome in the reading. Questions of tone and attitude will become more insistent in oral performance. Thus, it is advisable to work toward a reading performance as a final check on the degree to which we have mastered situation, ideas, images, attitudes, and music. An expert may be able to read through a piece of piano music and hear in his mind a perfect performance of it. Most of us need to tap out the notes before we can grasp melodies, harmonies, and rhythms with any sureness. Reading poetry aloud helps us to establish our grasp of it—especially if a patient and knowledgable teacher is there to correct our performance and encourage us to try again.

One last piece of advice, in the form of some lines
by Antonio Machado, translated by Robert Bly:*

> People possess four things
> that are no good at sea
> anchor, rudder, oars
> and the fear of going down.

* Reprinted by permission of the translator, Robert Bly.